THE Impressionists

THE
Impressionists
BOOK OF DAYS
❖
A sumptuous collection
of the artists, their paintings
and their lives

CHARTWELL
BOOKS, INC.

IMPRESSIONISM was the artistic phenomenon of the 19th century. Art was changed forever; although the ideas began in France, they gradually rippled out to touch artists all over the western world and transform the way we look at the world. What we now call Impressionism evolved from the work of a group of disparate artists all with their own theories. They fought and agreed, influenced and argued with each other, and banded together in the face of ridicule to exhibit their work. Although they were a distinct group for only a decade, from 1874 to 1884, their effect on the tradition of western art was formidable. Cézanne, Degas, Manet, Monet, Pissarro, Sisley, Renoir, Morisot, Cassatt, Bazille and Boudin all came from very different backgrounds, even from very different places. What they shared was the desire

66

One must be of one's time and paint what one sees.
MANET

99

Portable Paint

Painting in the open, one of the basic tenets of Impressionism, only really became possible after the invention of weatherproof, easily portable metal paint tubes in the 1840s.

IMPRESSION: SUNRISE (1872)
Claude Monet

to throw off the shackles of tradition, to paint contemporary subjects and to confront the problem of capturing the fleeting moment. Their technique was to paint directly outside, *en plein air, to use short sharp brush strokes to capture the impression of a scene before it changed. Landscape and figures in a landscape provided their favourite subject; the play of light on water in particular attracted them as a metaphor for the transient.*

Such revolutionary pictures were rejected out of hand by the Salon, although some were hung in the Salon des Refusés, notably Manet's Déjeuner sur l'Herbe. Despairing of ever finding a place to show their work, the painters decided to organise themselves. In December 1873, they formed the Société Anonyme Cooperative des Artistes, Peintres, Sculpteurs, Graveurs etc. and held their own exhibition on 15 April 1874 in the empty studios of the photographer Nadar on the Boulevard des Capucines in Paris. Claude Monet showed his picture Impression: Sunrise (1872). The critic Louis Leroy seized upon this, and used its title to make a sarcastic headline for his review: Exhibition of the Impressionists. The name was to stick, although they were also called Les Intransigents. The exhibition was the target of incredibly vitriolic attacks.

The artists were treated 'like lepers or beggars' according to Pissarro, their sanity was called into question, their work was vilified as pointless daubs, sloppy, slipshod and unfinished. This did not deter them from exhibiting again in 1876, 1877, (when they proudly adopted their derogatory nickname as their official title), 1879, 1880, 1881, 1882 and 1884. Impressionism made it possible for the Neo-Impressionists, Seurat and Signac, to evolve their theories of colour and line and was the foundation on which Post-Impressionists van Gogh and Gauguin based their work. Monet was its cornerstone and

Pissarro its most constant disciple but each artist in this book made their own unique contribution to the movement that gave birth to modern art.

January

ÉDOUARD MANET

1832 - 1883

ÉDOUARD MANET was born in 1832 into a wealthy bourgeois Parisian family. His father was a high-ranking civil servant and his mother a society hostess whose glittering salons attracted artists and poets. Young Manet showed little academic aptitude but a talent for drawing. His father sent him away to sea at the age of 16, but when he returned he went to Thomas Couture's studio where he studied for six years.

Manet was a consummate technician. He painted all kinds of pictures – portraits, landscapes, still lifes, and made prints and lithographs and etchings. Although the Impressionists moved him to lighten his palette, and make more naturalistic paintings, he was essentially a studio artist.

Throughout his career Manet was cast as an aristocratic rebel, although what he really wanted was success and acceptance by the establishment. It was his genuine desire to depict modern life that put him far ahead of the game. When *Déjeuner sur l'Herbe* was shown in the Salon des Refusés in 1863, with its notorious nude picnicker, critics could not reconcile the classical composition with the contemporary setting and characters, and it enjoyed a *succès de scandale*. Manet had studied past masters thoroughly and used the techniques to paint modern life.

His final masterpiece, *The Bar at the Folies Bergère* (1881) united his artistic intentions and ambition for public honours. Painted from sketches made *in situ*, the picture is lit by that most modern of inventions, electric light. Manet was at last awarded a second class medal by the Salon. It was just in time; he was suffering from *locomotor ataxia*, the disease which attacks the central nervous system, and he died, in great pain, on 30 April 1883.

THE BAR AT THE FOLIES BERGERE *Édouard Manet*

ulevard des Italiens

1

2

3

4

5

6

7

NOTES

> "
> *P*ainting begins with Manet.
> PAUL GAUGUIN
> "

MANET was a consummate *flâneur*, a sophisticated stroller of the boulevards, with impeccable taste in clothes, perfect manners, ironic wit and an eye for cool, detached observation of the passing scene.

JANUARY

8
9
1 0
1 1
1 2
1 3
1 4

NOTES

Music in the Tuileries was painted in 1862. Manet worked in his studio from sketches made *en plein air*. The picture, which shows the *beau monde* listening to music in the park, provoked uproar and threats of violence when it was shown in 1863. The composition was controversial, as was the generous use of Naples Yellow and Cobalt Blue, two pigments that had just become available to artists. Manet himself can be seen in the picture; he is the second man from the left, dapper in his top hat and cane.

MANET was a friend of the decadent poet Baudelaire, and many of his paintings are an expression of the poet's idea of the 'heroism of modern life'.

Violets feature in Manet's stunning portrait of Berthe Morisot who introduced him to the lighter palette of the Impressionists. She later married his brother Eugène.

PEONIES were one of Manet's favourite flowers in his garden and he made several studies of them. Their loose blooms suited his open, relaxed brushwork technique.

MANET was very taken with the Japanese prints exhibited at the Exposition Universelle in 1867, and began his own collection. The influence of the bold simple lines, and flat areas of colour can be seen in his painting *The Fifer (1866)*.

JANUARY

15

16

17

18

19

1839 Cézanne *born*

20

21

NOTES

JANUARY
2 2
2 3 *1832* Manet *born* *1892 First* Pissarro *one man exhibition in Paris*
2 4
2 5
2 6
2 7
2 8
N O T E S

The Artist in Love

*I*n 1862, Manet married Suzanne Leenhoff, his mistress since 1849. Suzanne had taught piano to Manet's brothers, and in 1854 she went back home to Holland, where she bore a son, Léon. Although there is some doubt whether the father was Manet or his own father, Auguste, the marriage was happy.

Detail from MUSIC OF THE TUILERIES (1862)
Édouard Manet

29

1899 Sisley *dies*

30

31

NOTES

66

*In beginning a picture,
he could never say
how it would come out.*
ÉMILE ZOLA

99

MANET had always admired Velásquez, and painted several Spanish pictures, including *The Spanish Singer*, accepted by the Salon in 1861 and *The Dead Toreador*. He did not actually visit Madrid until 1865, staying only 10 days as he did not like the food or climate.

MANET'S father sent him on a six month trip to Rio de Janeiro to prepare him for a naval career. He spent most of the voyage sketching, concluded that a life on the ocean wave was a dull business and persuaded his father to let him study art.

> What a painter! He has everything, an intelligent mind, an impeccable eye, and what a hand!
>
> PAUL SIGNAC

ABSINTHE, *la fée verte*, the green fairy, was the addictive hallucinogenic drink that maddened and enslaved. Artists, poets and writers alike chronicled its devastating effect: Manet's first major work, *The Absinthe Drinker (1859)* was rejected by the Salon, partly because of its subject matter.

February

PAUL CÉZANNE

1839-1906

PAUL CÉZANNE was born in Aix-en-Provence 1839, the son of a domineering and dictatorial father who did not marry his mother until 1844. Young Cézanne was expected to study law and join his father's prosperous banking business, but he was so unenthusiastic and dilatory that he was finally allowed to go to Paris to study art. Rejected by the École des Beaux Arts, he studied at the Académie Suisse instead. Here he met Pissarro, who befriended the intense, unsophisticated southerner and persuaded him to lighten his palette and work outside.

Cézanne feared and despised his father, considering him to be a philistine moneygrabber, but his father's fortune meant that he could concentrate on his art without financial worries. His output was prodigious – he painted mostly landscapes and still lifes, with some portraits – and most of the work was done in Provence. He exhibited at the Salon des Refusés in 1863 and the Impressionist exhibitions in 1874 and 1877, but his work was badly received.

Cézanne was the archetypal tortured, misunderstood artist and loner. Hypersensitive, bitter, intelligent, short-tempered, thin-skinned, misanthropic, jealous and contemptuous of most other artists, reclusive and eccentric, he felt himself unloved, unappreciated and an outcast. His isolation drove him to concentrate on his art, a never-ending search to translate nature in all its aspects into art. He died on October 22 1906 of pneumonia after being caught in a storm while out painting.

RED EARTH

COBALT BLUE

ULTRAMARINE

PRUSSIAN BLUE

EMERALD GREEN

VIRIDIAN

ZINC WHITE

IVORY BLACK

CHROME YELLOW

NAPLES YELLOW

YELLOW OCHRE

VERMILION

PIERROT AND HARLEQUIN *Paul Cézanne*

" CÉZANNE SPEAKING "

To paint a picture means making a composition...
The aptest qualification for fine artistic
conception is greatness of character.

———— ○ ————

Let us read nature.
Let us express our impressions and
experiences in an aesthetic both personal
and traditional.

———— ○ ————

I wanted to make impressions
into something as solid and permanent
as the art in museums.

———— ○ ————

Two things matter in a painter: his eye and his mind.
The two must give mutual support.
Both need to be trained: the eye by studying nature, the mind
by an orderly logical approach to impressions and experience.

———— ○ ————

There is neither line nor modelling, there is only contrast.
Once the colours are at their richest, the form will be at its fullest.

FEBRUARY
1
2
3
4
5
6
7
NOTES

FEBRUARY

8	
9	
10	
11	
12	
13	
14	

NOTES

'Look at Ste Victoire. What a sweep. What a commanding thirst for sunshine! And what melancholy in the evening when all that heaviness settles upon it.' Mont Ste-Victoire, north east of Aix-en-Provence, appeared throughout in Cézanne's work, making its debut in *The Cutting (1870)* but came to dominate his mature period. Altogether, he painted 30 oils and 45 watercolours of the mountain.

> 66
>
> *Nature is always the same but nothing of it remains, nothing of what appears to us. Our art must register the quivering of its duration with the elements, and the appearances of all its changes.*
>
> PAUL CÉZANNE
>
> 99

> 66
>
> *Courage, then, once again! Take up your brush once more and give your imagination free rein. I believe in you.*
>
> ÉMILE ZOLA
>
> 99

> 66
>
> *However does he do it? The moment he dabs two touches of paint on a canvas, the result is brilliant.*
>
> PIERRE-AUGUSTE RENOIR
>
> 99

> 66
>
> *Nature should be treated as cylinders, spheres and cones. It should all be aligned in correct perspective so that every side of an object or surface tends towards a central point.*
>
> PAUL CÉZANNE
>
> 99

FEBRUARY

15

16

17

18

20

1885 Whistler *gives the* Ten O' Clock Lecture

21

NOTES

POMMES ET ORANGES
Paul Cézanne

'I should like to astonish Paris with an apple,' wrote Cézanne in his poem of 1895, *Hannibal's Dream*. He painted more still lifes than any of his Impressionist colleagues and preferred fruit – 'more loyal' – to flowers. 'When you translate the skin of a beautiful peach, or the melancholy of an old apple, you sense their mutual reflections, the same mild shadows of relinquishment, the same loving sun, the same recollections of dew.'

ÉZANNE loved his native Provence, which provided the inspiration for most of his work. He felt *gauche* and *outré* in Paris, the sophisticated nerve centre of the art world, although he studied there for eight years.

ÉZANNE'S redoubtable father, Louis-Auguste, was a successful hatter who went on to establish a very profitable bank. Cézanne was obliged to work there himself in 1861. He wrote this irreverant couplet in one of the ledgers: *'Cézanne le banquier ne voit sans frémir/ Derrière son comptoir naître un peintre à venir.'* *'Old Banker Cézanne shudders and quakes/ Behind his counter, a painter awakes.'*

FEBRUARY
22
23
24
25
1841 Pierre-Auguste Renoir *born*   **26**
27
28
NOTES

LES JOUEURS DE CARTES
Paul Cézanne

The Artist in Love

Cézanne met Hortense Fiquet, seamstress, bookbinder and artist's model in 1869 when she was 19 and he was 30. They had a son, Paul, in 1872, but Cézanne kept his family a secret from his father until 1886, when the couple were finally married. It was not a happy marriage, and Hortense and young Paul spent much of the time in Paris while Cézanne worked in Provence. A mysterious and passionate affair with a woman in Aix in 1885 came to nothing.

ÉMILE Zola, the great French writer, was a schoolmate of Cézanne's at the College Bourbon in Aix and encouraged the artist to come to Paris. The friendship ended in 1886 when Zola published *L'Oeuvre*, which featured Claude Lantier, a suicidal genius and failed painter. Cézanne believed that Zola had based the character on him.

FEBRUARY
29
N O T E S

AFTER much experimenting, Cézanne perfected a technique of short, precise parallel brushstrokes. This enabled him to control and construct his paintings very precisely.

CÉZANNE'S first love was poetry. He was no mean poet himself but his hero was Charles Baudelaire, author of the sensational collection of poems, *Les Fleurs du Mal* (1857).

March

ALFRED SISLEY

1839 - 1899

ALFRED SISLEY was born in Paris in 1839 into an English family living in France. After a false start in the family business, his father indulged him in his artistic ambitions and in 1862 he enrolled at Gleyre's studio where he met Monet, Renoir and Bazille. He formed part of the Barbizon school in Fontainebleau forest, but did not begin serious painting until after 1870, when his father's business failed, his generous allowance dried up and he was forced to paint to support himself and his family. Poverty prevented him travelling far, and most of his work was done along the banks of the Seine and at Moret-sur-Loing, near Fontainebleau forest, where he settled in 1879.

Sisley was greatly influenced by Monet, who inspired his love for landscapes, and Renoir, who persuaded him to lighten his palette. He developed his own gentle, harmonious, subtle style, a sort of English Impressionism, serene and dreamily melancholic. He exhibited in the Salon in 1866 and the first Impressionist exhibition but his work went largely unappreciated until after his death.

An agreeable, generous dilettante, dilatory student and good natured, witty flirt in his youth, Sisley was close to Monet and Renoir, no doubt because of his generous pocket as well as his gentle temperament. Sadly, he lacked their survival instincts and the grind of poverty and lack of recognition embittered him and finally wore him out. He lamented that 'never in his lifetime would a ray of glory ever shine on [his] art'. Monet was at his bedside when he died of throat cancer in 1899.

CHROME YELLOW

LOW OCHRE

LEAD WHITE

VORY BLACK

EMERALD GREEN

COBALT BLUE

PRUSSIAN BLUE

COBALT VIOLET

RED ALIZARIN LAKE

VERMILION

THE FLOODS AT PORT MARLY *Alfred Sisley*

MONET was a great influence on Sisley, whose landscapes may be read as a delicate echo of Monet's bold, vigorous versions. Inspired by Monet's enthusiasm for the area, Sisley worked at Marly and Louveciennes, and later stayed with Monet at Argenteuil.

The *Floods at Port Marly* (1876) was painted when Sisley's talent had come into full bloom. Its assured composition, understated colours and expert rendering of water exemplify his refined, sensitive technique.

SISLEY'S father William ran a very successful business exporting artificial flowers mostly to South America. The family had lived in France for many years.

MARCH
1
2
1895 Morisot *dies*
3
4
5
6
7
NOTES

MARCH

8

9

10

11

12

13

14

NOTES

SISLEY was intended to go into the family business, and was sent to England in 1857 to learn the ropes. However, he shunned office life in favour of days in the museums and art galleries of London, where he studied the work of Turner and Constable. In 1862, his father relented and allowed him to return to Paris and study art full time.

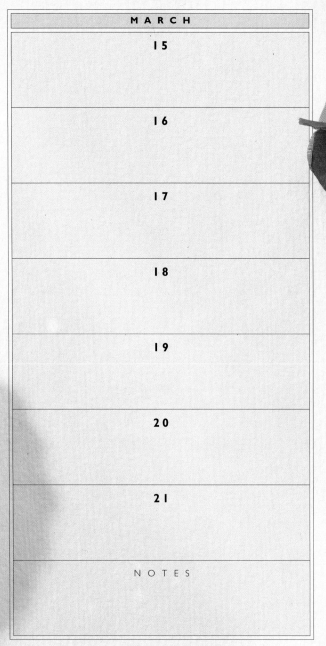

SISLEY'S work sold so badly that he rarely had enough money to eat. He was discreetly helped by M. Eugène Murer, the proprietor of a cake shop and restaurant in Auvers-sur-Oise. Unable to look on while poor Sisley starved, M. Murer often gave him meals in exchange for paintings.

MARCH

15

16

17

18

19

20

21

NOTES

IN 1863, Sisley, Monet, Renoir and Bazille spent the summer in Fontainebleau, staying first at Chailly-en-Bière then at Marlotte, at the famous Auberge de la Mère Anthony. Renoir painted a delightful picture of Sisley and Monet at the auberge, flirting with the landlady's dark-eyed daughter, Nana. Sisley returned often to Fontainebleau and painted *The Garde-Champêtre in the Forest of Fontainebleau* in 1870. The Sisleys later settled near Fontainebleau at Moret-sur-Loing.

MARCH

22

23

24

25

1841 Renoir *born*

26

27

28

NOTES

ALTHOUGH he lived in France all his life, Sisley never relinquished his British nationality and so was spared the obligation of military duty in the Franco-Prussian war. He was in England between 1857 and 1862 working in his father's business, and again in 1871 and 1874, when he painted at Hampton Court and various London suburbs.

LONDON. — St-James's Palace.

320

Ateliers and Académies

*T*wo independent studios were the breeding grounds for Impressionism. Charles Gleyre, a Swiss born painter and advocate of *plein air* taught Bazille, Monet, Renoir, Sisley and Whistler in his atelier in the rue Notre Dame des Champs. Over on the Quai des Orfèvres, the Académie Charles Suisse was the training ground for Pissarro and Cézanne.

BOATS AT THE LOCK AT BOUGIVAL (1873)
Alfred Sisley

The Artist in Love

*A*fter some harmless youthful flirtation with the pretty models who flocked to join the young artists in Fontainebleau forest, Sisley married in 1867. Renoir painted a delightful portrait of the young couple for the Salon of 1868. They had two children.

66

*W*hat could be *more beautiful indeed than the summer sky, with its wispy clouds idly floating across the blue.*
SISLEY

99

MARCH

29

1891 Seurat *dies*

30

31

NOTES

Café Society

*I*n the late 19th century, Paris was the centre of the art world, and many of its artists (except the women) met to argue and discuss their work in its elegant cafés. Manet led the group that included Sisley, Degas, Cézanne and Renoir, who met at the Café Guerbois in the Grand rue de Batignolles. After 1875 the Café Nouvelle Athènes in the Place Pigalle was the Impressionists meeting place.

April

BERTHE MORISOT

1841 - 1895

BERTHE MORISOT was born at Bourges in 1841 into the wealthy, *haut bourgeois* family of a government administrator. The Morisots moved to Paris in 1855 and in 1857 Berthe and her sister Edma were sent to lessons at the studio of Joseph-Benoit Guichard, an excellent art teacher and champion of women's education. Guichard quickly realised their potential talent and warned their mother of the danger of their becoming real artists. However, Madame Morisot supported her daughters and their father built them a studio in the huge garden of the family house at Passy. The girls studied in the Louvre and with Corot and had works in the Salons of 1864 and 1865. In 1867, Berthe was introduced to Édouard Manet, an artist from the same upper class milieu as the Morisots, whose brother Eugène she married in 1874.

In spite of being regularly accepted by the Salon, Morisot enthusiastically threw her lot in with the Impressionists and became central to the movement, often being described as the 'quintessential Impressionist'. Her 'rainbow' palette, preference for painting *en plein air* and feathery brushstroke technique were hallmarks of the style. Convention circumscribed her subject matter, limiting her to domestic interiors and family portraits , although she enjoyed more freedom in the country where she could work unchaperoned.

Morisot was admired by all the Impressionists, but was particularly close to Renoir. When she died in 1895, he was painting with Cézanne in Provence. He immediately closed his paintbox, and caught the next train to Paris to comfort and solace her daughter Julie.

WOMAN AND CHILD IN A GARDEN AT BOUGIVAL *Berthe Morisot*

The impossibility of being a woman artist

Morisot was very frustrated at the barriers women had to surmount just to have the same opportunities to paint as men. She poured out her feelings in her diary in January 1879.

'What I long for is the freedom of going about alone, of coming and going, of sitting in the seats of the Tuileries, and especially in the Luxembourg, of stopping and looking at the artistic shops, of entering churches and museums, of walking about the old streets at night; that's what I long for; and that's the freedom without which one cannot become a real artist. Do you imagine that I get much good from what I see, chaperoned as I am, and when, in order to go to the Louvre, I must wait for my carriage, my lady companion and family?... This is one of the principal reasons why there are no female artists.'

APRIL

1

2

3

4

5

6

7

NOTES

LIKE most of the other Impressionists, Morisot spent summers on the Normandy and Brittany coast where, liberated from the restrictions of town etiquette, she could paint out in the open. Dieppe, Beuzeval, Fécamp, Les Petites-Dalles, Boulogne, Lorient and Cherbourg all feature in Morisot pictures.

"

She would vanish for entire days among the cliffs, pursuing one motif after another, according to the hour and the slant of the sun.

TIBURCE MORISOT

"

La Porte et le Bou...

APRIL
8
9
10
11
12
13
14
NOTES

IN 1872 Manet painted one of his masterpieces, a portrait of Berthe Morisot wearing violets. In gratitude for her posing, he painted a charming little still life of a bunch of violets with a thank-you note.

Morisot and the Manet brothers

Morisot met Édouard Manet in 1867. She was a great influence on his work, persuading him to lighten his palette. They became very good friends: she posed for several of his pictures, including *The Balcony* (1868-9). There may have been a decorous infatuation, but Morisot married Manet's brother Eugène in 1874 and bore him a daughter, Julie, in 1878.

APRIL
15
1874 First Impressionist exhibition
16
17
18
19
20
21
NOTES

APRIL
22
23
24
25
26
27
1888 Cézanne *marries*
28
NOTES

66

N*o one represents Impressionism with more refined talent or with more authority than Morisot.*

GUSTAVE GEFFROY

99

66

T*all and slender, of great distinction of manner, an artist of delicate and subtle talent...*

HENRI DE REGNIER, CRITIC

99

APRIL
29
30
1883 Manet *dies*
NOTES

MORISOT'S subject range was restricted by the conventions of a woman's place, so she turned to her immediate family as models, which meant that children featured a lot. Edma Morisot and her daughter Jeanne sat for *Woman and Child seated in a Field*, shown at the first Impressionist exhibition. Morisot's favourite model was her own daughter Julie, often shown playing with her father.

> 66
>
> *A*re you sure that you will not come to curse the day when art, having gained admission to your home, now so respectable and peaceful, will become the sole arbiter of the fate of two of your children?
>
> JOSEPH GUICHARD TO MME MORISOT
>
> 99

DRAWING was considered an essential part of girl's education as outlined by Jean-Jacques Rousseau in his influential novel *Émile* (1762). Art, culture and science were considered the province of men; watercolour painting and design were considered proper accomplishments for women. In Paris in 1869, there were 20 design schools for women but only seven for men. However, the École des Beaux Arts, the state art school, was not open to women students until 1887, and then only after a great deal of vociferous complaint by women artists.

MORISOT'S intimate portraits of women (often her own sisters or nieces) showed them relaxed at their ease, with their natural props such as fans or mirrors. *At the Ball* (1875) shows Edma almost dominated by a large, beautiful fan.

May

FRÉDÉRIC BAZILLE

1841 - 1870

IVORY BLACK

RED EARTH

YELLOW OCHRE

JEAN-FRÉDÉRIC BAZILLE was born in 1841 into a rich Protestant family in Montpelier, south west France. He had a happy, secure childhood, and developed an early obsession with art and spent his leisure hours at drawing, painting and modelling lessons. He also spent a lot of time at the house of the wealthy art collector Alfred Bruyas, where the young Bazille admired works by Delacroix and Courbet. In 1862, Gaston Bazille allowed his son to go to Paris to study art, as long as he kept up his medical studies. Bazille joined the group at the Gleyre studio, where he met Monet, Renoir and Sisley.

Tall, handsome, wealthy, generous and popular, Bazille worked hard at his studies. He spent summers in Fontainebleau with the Barbizon school and travelled to Normandy with Monet. He appears in many of his friends' pictures (saving them paying a model), gave money to Monet, shared his studio with Renoir, and often bought his friends' work. He wrote home regularly to report his own progress and enthuse about the talent of his colleagues. Sadly, Bazille's promising career was cut short when he was killed in the Franco-Prussian war.

COBALT BLUE

EMERALD GREEN

ULTRAMARINE

LEAD WHITE

THE FAMILY REUNION *Frédéric Bazille*

TO the southerner Bazille, the lush greenery of northern forests and the light sparkle of the Seine were a diverting change from the hot brightness of his native land.

The Landscape Painter's Paradise

In the early 1860's, Renoir, Sisley, Monet, Bazille formed part of the Barbizon school, a group of artists who worked in the forest of Fontainebleau, following the example of older artists like Daubigny, Millet and Diaz de Peña. They stayed at cheap auberges in the villages of Chailly-en Bière, Marlotte or Barbizon, which gave its name to their 'school'.

> ❝
> *It is full of light and sunshine. Bazille is looking for what we have always wanted to find: how to paint a figure out in the open. This time I think he really has succeeded.*
> BERTHE MORISOT
> ❞

MAY
1
2
3
4
5
6
7

In one of Bazille's many letters home, he roundly blamed the Impressionist's lack of success on one of the directors of the Hanging Committee of the Salon, who decided which painting would be exhibited every year. 'It is Monsieur Gérôme who has done the damage. He has treated us like a gang of lunatics and has said that he believes it to be his duty to do everything in his power to prevent our painters from exhibiting.'

Salon des Refusés

In 1863, more than 4,000 artists had their work rejected by a particularly fierce Salon jury. Outraged, they turned to the Emperor Napoleon III, who established a second exhibition space, the Salon des Refusés, where paintings thought too controversial for the Salon could be shown. Manet, Pissarro, Whistler and Cézanne were represented. The Salon des Refusés broke the stranglehold of the academic, conservative Salon and is often seen by critics as signalling the beginning of modern art.

BAZILLE'S father was a wealthy man who owned several vineyards and was senator of the Hérault département of south west France. He was generous to his son and Bazille kept in close contact throughout his tragically short artistic career. In 1867, he painted *Family Reunion*, a group portrait of the members of his family posed on the terrace of their home. It was exhibited in the 1868 Salon.

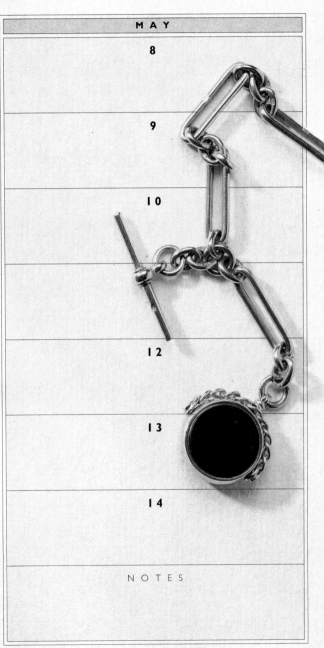

MAY

8

9

1 0

1 2

1 3

1 4

NOTES

LIKE all wars, the Franco-Prussian war of 1870-71 cut a swathe through a generation of young men. Monet, who had done his military service, avoided the war along with Pissarro (who was too old) and Cézanne. Renoir served in a cavalry regiment, Manet joined the National Guard, Degas volunteered for the artillery, as did Bazille, in spite of his father's arrangements to keep him out. He was killed on active service on 28 November 1870.

BAZILLE'S family wanted him to be a doctor, and he was only allowed to study art if he kept up his medical studies at the same time. His medical expertise came in useful when he had to treat Monet who had injured his leg in Fontainebleau.

One of the most significant aspects of Impressionism is the lightening of the palette, hitherto kept dark in the tradition of the old masters. Impressionist colours were yellow, orange, vermilion, crimson, violet, blue and green.

MAY
1 5
1886 Eighth and last Impressionist exhibition *begins*
1 6
1 7
1 8
1 9
2 0
2 1
NOTES

MAY	
22	
	1844 Cassatt *born*
23	
24	
26	
27	
28	
NOTES	

The Father of Modern Landscape

This was how Manet described the Dutch born Johann Barthold Jongkind (1819-1891) who pioneered the lively broken brushwork that characterized Impressionism. After studying at the Hague, Jongkind went to France in 1846, spending most of his time in Brittany and Normandy. He met Boudin at Le Havre in 1862 and the pair spent the next few summers painting and sketching at Le Havre and Honfleur. Jongkind's ideas influenced Boudin, who in turn influenced Monet.

IN May 1864, Bazille travelled to Normandy, with Monet as his guide. Monet introduced him to Rouen, Le Havre and Honfleur. They based themselves at the inn at Saint-Simeon farm, where Courbet, Jongkind and Boudin used to meet, punctuating their painting day with generous lunches of eggs, cream and cider.

LOUIS-EUGÈNE BOUDIN

1824 - 1898

BOUDIN was born in Honfleur in 1824, the son of a sailor. He ran a picture framing business in Le Havre, and painted in his spare time as a pupil of Eugène Isabey. One of Boudin's distinguished customers, Millet, offered encouragement and he went to Paris to study. He was an indifferent student, and came back because he wanted to paint outdoors. Modest and self-deprecatory ('I lack verve of execution'), Boudin was the timid harbourer of revolutionary ideas. He was convinced that it was essential to retain 'one's first impression' and to paint outside, in front of the subject to pursue the 'perfection of fleeting colour and light'. He meticulously recorded these ideas in a set of immaculate notebooks, just as he noted down the date, time and wind direction on the margins of all his paintings. Baudelaire, staying with his widowed mother in Honfleur, was very impressed with Boudin's work, and maintained that you could tell the season, time and windiness just by looking at one of Boudin's pieces, regardless of the neat captions. The young Monet, who met Boudin in 1856, was electrified by these ideas which embodied the main principles of Impressionism. Boudin showed work at the 1874 Impressionist exhibition, but his lack of self confidence prevented him from joining the great masters.

A BOUDIN MUSEUM in Honfleur celebrates the work of its native son.

Boudin's influence on Monet

'Suddenly a veil was torn away. I had understood – I had realized what painting could be. By the single example of this painter devoted to his art with such independence. My destiny as a painter opened out to me.' So Claude Monet paid tribute to Boudin's profound influence on him, even though he had despised the modest seascapist's efforts to begin with. Monet took Boudin's diffidently expressed ideas and expanded them into a full scale artistic theory - Impressionism.

66

Everything that is painted directly and on the spot always has a force, a power, a vivacity of touch that cannot be recreated in the studio.
BOUDIN

99

THE BEACH AT LOW TIDE, DEAUVILLE
Eugène Boudin

AT the beginning of the 19th century, Honfleur became something of an artist's haven: Courbet, Corot, Isabey and Bonington all painted seascapes there. To Boudin it was home, Jongkind, Bazille and Monet all visited and painted there.

> 66
> *Tones must be clear and fresh, brilliant if possible.*
> BOUDIN
> 99

BOUDIN stayed faithful to his preferred subject, the beaches and seascapes of the Normandy coast.

MAY
29
30
3 1
NOTES

June

PIERRE-AUGUSTE RENOIR

1841-1919

PIERRE-AUGUSTE RENOIR was born in Limoges, in 1841, the son of a tailor. The family moved to Paris when Renoir was three years old. Apprenticed as a porcelain painter at the age of 13, young Renoir spent his lunchtimes studying great works in the Louvre, and saved up to pay to study at the École des Beaux Arts, where he studied with Charles Gleyre alongside a constellation of budding Impressionist artists such as Monet, Sisley and Bazille. In the summer, they moved to the forest of Fontainebleau to paint direct from nature. Renoir struggled cheerfully in great poverty, but was helped by wealthy friends such as Bazille, whose studio he shared.

Lack of funds prevented Renoir from travelling - although he did sail down the Seine to Le Havre − but he found suitable subjects wherever he was, as he preferred to paint people − moving, flirting, dancing, playing, eating, enjoying themselves. His great decade was between 1872 and 1883, although his work was dismissed by many contemporary critics as 'chaotic and disorderly'. Never a revolutionary, Renoir exhibited his work at the Salon and the Impressionist exhibitions and became one of the lucky few artists whose work eventually found favour during his lifetime, giving him financial security and the means to travel to Algiers, Italy, Holland and Germany. He never stopped painting, even when suffering from rheumatoid arthritis, when his hands were so deformed, the brush had to be tied on. He died on December 3rd 1919. As his works show, Renoir was a celebrator of life, the uncomplicated chronicler of *joie-de-vivre* whose work never fails to lift the spirit.

VERMILION

RED ALIZARIN LAKE

COBALT BLUE

YELLOW OCHRE

NAPLES YELLOW

VIRIDIAN

ÉMERALD GREEN

ULTRAMARINE

ZINC WHITE

CHROME YELLOW

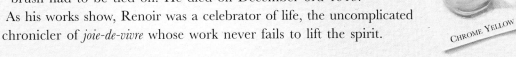

UN JEUNE FILLE *Pierre-Auguste Renoir*

JUNE
1
2
3
4
5
6
7
NOTES

RENOIR SPEAKING

"

*For me a picture has to be something
pleasant, delightful and pretty – yes, pretty.
There are enough unpleasant things in the world
without us producing even more.*

———○———

*The constant urge is to look for inspiration in art!
For my part, I am content to demand
just one thing of a masterpiece: enjoyment.*

———○———

*Although we don't eat every day,
I am quite cheerful.*

———○———

*Nature leads the artist into loneliness;
I want to remain among people.*

———○———

*If God had not created womens' breasts,
I may not have become a painter.*

La Loge was painted in 1874, in time for the Impressionists first exhibition, where it was roundly scorned. It's hard to see why such an unaffectedly beautiful picture could provoke outrage, but it sold for only 425 francs, which Renoir needed desperately to pay the rent. The models for the picture were Edmond Renoir, the painter's brother, and a little girl called Nini Lopez.

> **"**
>
> I *despise all living painters except Monet and Renoir.*
>
> PAUL CÉZANNE
>
> **"**

JUNE
8
9
1 0
1 1
1 2
1 3
1 4
NOTES

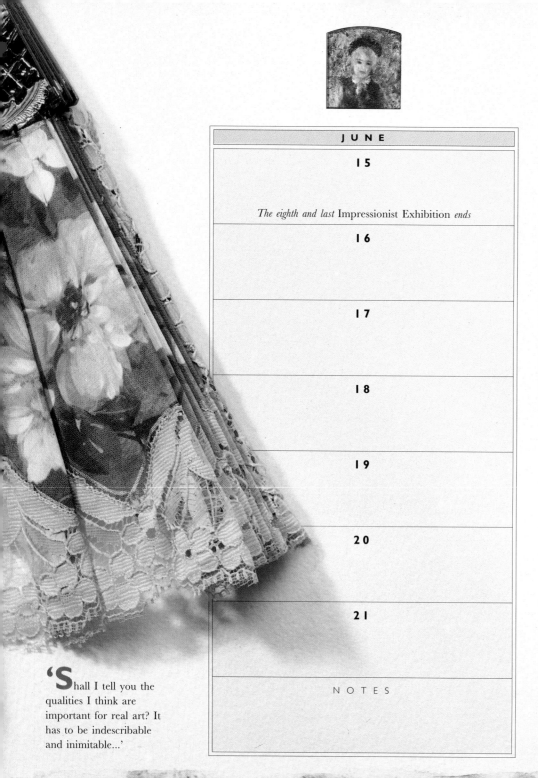

JUNE

15

The eighth and last Impressionist Exhibition *ends*

16

17

18

19

20

21

NOTES

The Apprentice

When he was thirteen years old, Renoir became an apprentice porcelain painter. He was so good that his workmates nicknamed him 'Monsieur Rubens'. Four years later, machines made his work redundant, and he painted church banners, ladies' fans and shop blinds instead.

RENOIR was a popular member of the café society of Bohemian Paris, which was concentrated around the Butte of Montmartre, the artist's quarter. He would set out his easel among the tables and paint his friends at play. *Le Moulin de la Galette* (1877) is the glorious celebration of an impromptu outdoor party.

'**S**hall I tell you the qualities I think are important for real art? It has to be indescribable and inimitable...'

JUNE
22
23
24
25
26
27
28
NOTES

66

*T*he summer
shades of the Bergen Tulip
take my breath away. . .

99

RENOIR was eighty when he died in 1919. In sixty years of painting, he had produced around 6,000 works – only Picasso has been more prolific. Renoir's great decade of painting was between 1872 and 1883, although this work was dismissed by many of his contemporary critics.

'When I paint flowers, my mind has a rest...' These were Renoir's dying words about a still-life arrangement he had been working on. Flowers feature throughout Renoir's work, but towards the end of his life, he used flower painting to explore techniques.

CHILDREN often starred in, or formed a major part of, a Renoir scene. He was a master at capturing the rosy sheen of an infant cheek and the artlessness of a child's posture without patronising or trivialising his subjects.

JUNE

29

30

NOTES

JEAN RENOIR, the artist's second son, went on to 'paint in light', becoming one of the century's most important – and painterly – film directors.

LUNCHEON OF THE BOATING PARTY
Pierre Auguste Renoir

FEW artists celebrated the simple pleasures of life more enchantingly than Renoir. *The Luncheon of the Boating Party* (1881) showed Renoir's friends and fellow artists enjoying a relaxed lunch after their exertions on the river.

The Artist in Love

Renoir met Aline Charigot in 1880. She is the pretty girl with the poppies in her hat and a little dog on the table before her in *The Luncheon of the Boating Party*. Their son Pierre was born in 1885, but they didn't get married until 1890. Jean was born in 1894 and Claude ('Coco') in 1901. Aline died in 1915.

July

GEORGES SEURAT

1859 - 1891

RED ALIZARIN LAKE

COBALT VIOLET

GEORGES SEURAT was born in 1859 at La Villette, near Paris, into a prosperous family. After studying at the École des Beaux Arts and in the Louvre, Seurat was able to concentrate on his work, particularly his scientific theories of art; family wealth meant that he could dedicate himself to his art without financial worry.

ZINC WHITE

CADMIUM YELLOW

He was a superb and original draughtsman and his black and white drawings are masterly. Irritated by what he conceived to be the impulsive, unstructured self-indulgence of the Impressionists, Seurat aimed to codify a theory that would explain the effects that the Impressionists achieved by intuition. His ideas were taken up by Pissarro, who encouraged him to exhibit his masterpiece *La Grande Jatte* at the last Impressionist exhibition of 1886, but the other Impressionists were hostile.

Seurat's theories influenced Gauguin, van Gogh, Toulouse-Lautrec and Matisse, but his faithful disciple was Paul Signac. He died in 1891 in mysterious circumstances: either of meningitis, an untreated throat infection or, as Signac maintained, of overwork and disappointment at the unenthusiastic reception of his ideas.

VERMILION

COBALT BLUE

VIRIDIAN

ULTRAMARINE

EMERALD GREEN

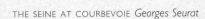

THE SEINE AT COURBEVOIE *Georges Seurat*

JULY

1	
2	
3	
4	
5	
6	
7	
NOTES	

JULY
8
9
1 0
1830 Pissarro *born*
1 1
1834 Whistler *born*
1 2
1 3
1 4
N O T E S

'The most beautiful drawings by a painter in existence.' Paul Signac
    Seurat's preferred drawing medium was black *conté* crayon. In the early 1880s he concentrated on this aspect of his art, making over 400 black and white drawings, notable for their sensitive lyrical qualities.

LA GRANDE JATTE (1884-1886) is Seurat's masterpiece. It shows Sunday afternoon on the island of Grand Jatte, a popular resort on the Seine. It is made up of uniform sized dots meticulously placed side by side giving the overall impression of the shimmering heat of a still summer day. Paradoxically, the ceaseless vibration between the spots of colour produce a calm, static picture.

JULY

15

16

1892 Monet *marries* Alice Hochschede

17

1903 Whistler *dies*

18

19

1834 Degas *born*

20

21

NOTES

Colour Theory

Seurat's colour theory was based on the works of the physicists Eugène Chevreul and Ogden Rood, author of *Modern Chromatics* (1879). According to Chevreul, colours can be divided into two groups: primary colours, red, yellow and blue, and secondary colours, green, orange and purple, which are made by mixing primary colours. Secondary colours look stronger when placed next to a primary colour not used to make them: orange next to blue, green next to red and purple next to yellow. These pairs of colours are called complementary colours. Seurat used complementary colours to create the luminous vibrancy which characterises his paintings.

JULY

22

23

24

25

26

27

28

NOTES

Line and Tone Theory

Seurat was working towards a theory of composition that would produce harmony and guarantee a specific mood. He theorised that the artist could create certain moods by manipulating line, tone and colour. For a cheerful effect, you need luminous tone, warm dominant colour and lines rising above the horizontal; for a calm scene, equal balance of tone and warm and cool colour and horizontal lines are necessary; and a sad mood calls for dark tones, cold colours and lines going downwards.

Divisionism

Divisionism is the method of achieving colour effects by placing small patches of colour on the canvas closely side by side so that they react together to give the desired effect. Impressionism used the technique instinctively but Seurat formalised the theory, calling the result 'optical mixture' supposing that the desired colour effect would be mixed by the eye and brain of the beholder standing a certain distance from the picture. It was the practical Pissarro who calculated that the proper distance to stand is three times the diagonal measurement of the painting. In reality, the patches of colour are not mixed together by the observer's eye, but vibrate together to give a shimmering effect.

BETWEEN 1913 and 1919, Signac was living in Antibes, and discovering unspoilt Mediterranean villages such as St Tropez. This was where he met Matisse.

Pointillism

Pointillism was a term invented by the critic Félix Fénéon to describe Seurat's painting method. It describes the masses of tiny dots (points) used to make up the picture.

PAUL SIGNAC

1863 - 1935

PAUL SIGNAC was born in 1863. He began painting in 1882. After studying at the École des Beaux-Arts he met Seurat and became a committed follower of Seurat's ideas. Monet was also a great influence.

Signac was a prolific painter, tireless traveller and industrious writer. His book *From Eugéne Delacroix to Neo-Impressionism* (1889) attempted to trace the history of artistic theory of divisionism. He also wrote a book on the Dutch Impressionist Jongkind and in 1922 produced a treatise on water colour techniques. He was a co-founder, with Seurat, of the Salon des Independants.

After Seurat's death, Signac began to travel all over France from Brittany to Corsica, and visited Holland, Genoa, Venice and Constantinople. He painted constantly, becoming an excellent water colourist and his work improved as he expanded his vision beyond the narrow confines of Neo-Impressionism. In 1913, he went to the south of France, where he met Matisse on whose work he had a great influence. He died in 1935.

> *It is not a question of talent but of technique.*
>
> PAUL SIGNAC

JULY
29
30
31
NOTES

Salon des Indépendants

*I*n 1884, Seurat and Signac established
their own version of the Salon des Refusés.
Called the Salon des Indépendants, it began life
as little more than a collection of sheds in the
Tuileries gardens. There was no selection process:
artists paid to display their work, which had usually
been rejected by the Salon. The Salon des Indépendants
grew in influence and provided a showcase for the works
of the Post-Impressionists.

August

CLAUDE OSCAR MONET

1840-1926

CLAUDE OSCAR MONET was born in 1840 in Paris, but moved with his family to Le Havre. Idle at school, with a talent for drawing and caricature, he was influenced by the landscapists Boudin and Jongkind, but went on to become greater than either.

Monet was at the very centre of what was to become the Impressionist school. He studied at the Académie Suisse in 1859 alongside Pissarro and Cézanne and after his military service at Gleyre's Studio with Bazille, Sisley and Renoir. An outdoor man, he painted in the forest of Fontainebleau, on the banks of the Seine – he built a studio on a boat – and on the beaches of Normandy. It was his picture of dawn over Le Havre harbour, which he labelled *Impression: Sunrise* (1872) which was seized on by critics when it was exhibited in 1874 and gave its name to the movement as a whole.

A stranger to self-doubt, Monet was bold, energetic, cheerful and utterly committed to his art. Chronically in debt because of his refusal to starve in a garret, he was shamelessly ruthless, cunning and even unscrupulous when begging or borrowing money to live and paint and often ran away from his financial obligations. Fortunately, after a penurious start, Monet finally became successful and after 1890 he was able to buy his house at Giverny and concentrate on his serial paintings – one subject painted at different times of day and in different lights.

Monet remained committed to the ideas and intentions of Impressionism throughout his life. He died on December 5 1926.

WOMAN WITH PARASOL *Claude Monet*

M ONET liked to smoke. He preferred cigarettes as he worked and a pipe to relax with. Renoir painted a candid portrait of him puffing on his long stemmed pipe as he read a newspaper.

The Artist in Love

M onet married his mistress and model Camille Doncieux in 1870, after she had born him a son, Jean. After Camille's long illness and death in 1879 left him with two young sons to look after, he set up a *ménage* with art collector Ernest Hochschede, his wife Alice and their children. After Ernest's death, Monet married Alice in 1892. The second Mme Monet refused to allow any female models into the house.

AUGUST

1	
2	
3	
4	
5	
6	
7	

NOTES

'It took me some time to understand my water lilies ... I had planted them for the pleasure of it; I was growing them without thinking of painting them. A landscape does not get under your skin in one day. And then all of a sudden I had the revelation of how enchanting my pond was. I took up my palette. Since then, I've hardly had any other subject.' The waterlilies series was the last project that Monet undertook. He began in 1899, and was still working on the images at his death 27 years later.

ALTHOUGH he was born in Paris, Monet spent a carefree youth and adolescence at Le Havre, on the Normandy coast. His lifelong romance with light on water must have started here.

"
The Raphael of Water.
EDOUARD MANET
"

IN SPITE OF chronic financial troubles, Monet managed to travel quite extensively, visiting Holland, England and Italy. Each visit is documented by a series of pictures.

AUGUST
8
9
1 0
1 1
1 2
1 3
1 4
NOTES

AUGUST

15

16

17

18

19

20

21

NOTES

IN most of his figure painting, Monet posed his model with a parasol, which enabled him to have some control over the the fall and direction of light.

"

He is the painter of air and light, of affinities and reflexes, of clouds fleeing, of mists dissipating, of shafts of light displaced by the earth as it turns.

ROGER MARX
Gazette des Beaux Arts
June 1909

"

AUGUST

22
23
24
25
26
27
28
NOTES

Monet often used Paris fashion
plates as reference for his figure paintings.

MONET visited England at the turn of the century and was beguiled by the fog. He made several studies of the Thames bridges and the Houses of Parliament. He made several studies in pastels while waiting for his canvases to arrive from France. Although he had not used pastels for some time, he found them exactly right for capturing the all-enshrouding mists that hovered over London's river.

Plein Air

This term, French for open air, describes a painting done outside in the open air rather than in the studio from previous sketches.

MONET took outdoor painting so seriously that he had a trench dug in his garden so that he could stand at the correct height to his subject.

MONET 'liked flags very much', attracted to their dashing flow and movement. He used them in several pictures, especially the seaside ones and *Rue Montorgueil Decked Out with Flags* (1878).

> **"**
>
> *Monet is nothing but an eye – though God knows, what an eye!*
> PAUL CÉZANNE
>
> **"**

AUGUST
29
30
31
NOTES

MONET SPEAKING

I've always had a horror of theories. Mine is only the merit of having painted directly from nature, trying to convey my own impressions in the presence of fugitive effects.

———— ○ ————

Techniques will vary, art stays the same; it is a transportation of nature both forceful and sensitive.

The word Impressionist was created for him, and it fits him better than it does anyone else.

FELIX FENÉON (1888)

IN order to get nearer the water, in 1874 Monet commissioned a custom built boat to be his floating studio. It had a large cabin with a festive striped awning in front of it so he would be shaded from the sun as he painted. He moored at Argenteuil and other spots along the Seine. Other artists sometimes used it, although Berthe Morisot complained that it rocked about too much for her to settle down to work.

LA BARQUE BLEU
Claude Monet

September

JAMES ABBOTT McNEILL WHISTLER

1834 - 1903

RAW UMBER

WHISTLER was born in Lowell, Massachusetts, USA. He was sent to West Point Military Academy in 1851 but had no interest in a soldier's life and was discharged in 1854. After an unproductive year working for the Coastal Survey, where he had to engrave maps and plans, he begged an allowance from his family and went to live in Paris in 1855. In 1856, he joined Gleyre's studio where he met Courbet, who was to be a great influence. In 1860, he settled in London, but travelled to France frequently, spending the summer of 1865 at Trouville, painting seascapes with Courbet.

Whistler shared many of the Impressionists' aims – to capture the fleeting effects of light on water, the movement of waves and clouds – but rejected the *plein air* idea. And while Impressionism concentrated on the effects of sunlight, Whistler was intrigued by the behaviour of light at night time, dusk or dawn. His relationship with other Impressionists was cordial but distant. Degas admired his seascapes. He corresponded with Monet and Degas, who admired his Trouville landscapes, and met Renoir in 1881. He exhibited *White Girl* in the Salon of 1863, alongside Manet's *Déjeuner sur l'Herbe*. His close friendship with the poet Mallarmé, also a friend of Manet, Monet and Degas, brought the artists together.

An eccentric, flamboyant dandy, poseur and acerbic wit, Whistler cut a dashing bohemian swathe through society in both England and France.

As an outsider, he was able to bring artists from both countries together. He died in 1903 in London.

COBALT BLUE

ULTRAMARINE

EMERALD GREEN

ZINC WHITE

VERMILION

NAPLES YELLOW

IVORY BLACK

SYMPHONY IN BLUE AND PINK *James Whistler*

DURING the 1860s, Whistler came under the influence of Japanese art, copying Japanese line and proportion and adding oriental motifs such as fans and blossoms to his pictures. *The Princess from the Land of Porcelain* (1863-4) and *Caprice No 2 in Purple and Gold: The Golden Screen* (1864) are exquisite examples of obviously Japanese influenced art.

WHISTLER'S father was a railway engineer and in 1843 he took the family to St Petersburg where he was involved in the Moscow-St Petersburg Railway. The young Whistler had lessons in art and French, studied at the Imperial Art Academy and visited the Hermitage where he saw works by great masters. He was particularly influenced by Velásquez.

The Idler

*A*t Gleyre's studio, Whistler was nicknamed the 'Idle Apprentice'. He was the basis for the character of the same name in George du Maurier's novel of *la vie bohème*, *Trilby*, published in 1894.

SEPTEMBER

1	
2	
3	
4	
5	
6	
7	

NOTES

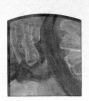

SEPTEMBER
8
9
10
11
12
13
14
NOTES

John Henry Twachtmann and The Ten

The ripples of Impressionism gradually spread as far as America via well-travelled Europhiles such as Childe Hassam and Mary Cassatt. In 1898, the artist John Henry Twachtmann founded as The Ten, a group of American artists who proclaimed themselves to be the representatives of Impressionism in the U.S.A. They were Frank Benson, Joseph de Camp, Thomas Dewing, Childe Hassam, Willard Metcalfe, Robert Reid, Edward E. Simmons, Edmund Tarbell, J. Alden Weir, William Merritt Chase and Twachtmann himself, a painter best known for his winter scenes reminiscent of the work of Monet and Sisley. Most of them had studied in Paris during the 1880s.

SEPTEMBER
15
16
17
18
19
20
21
NOTES

THE Ten O' Clock lecture, given on February 20 1885, was Whistler's defence of his own artistic theory and the artist's right to paint what he feels. In 1888, Mallarmé translated it into French and read it at one of Berthe Morisot's weekly salons.

WHISTLER'S first love was engraving and printing and he made over 400 etchings and 150 lithographs. Pissarro, no mean etcher himself, was very impressed with them and urged his son Lucien to go and see them when he was in London.

Art for Art's Sake

'*A*rt should be independent of all clap-trap – should stand alone, and appeal to the artistic sense of eye or ear, without confounding this with emotions entirely foreign to it, as devotion, pity, love, patriotism and the like. All these have no kind of concern with it, and that is why I insist on calling my works "arrangements" and "harmonies".'

WHISTLER

IN 1879, the Fine Art Society commissioned Whistler to make a series of etchings of Venice. While there, he made paintings and pastels as well, enough to hold two exhibitions on his return in 1880 and 1883.

SEPTEMBER

22

23

24

25

26

27

1917 Degas *dies*

28

NOTES

The Artist in Love

*W*histler's love life was notorious and he became a focus for admirers of both sexes. In 1860, Joanna Heffernan became his mistress and model and went to Trouville with him in 1865, but ran away with Courbet. In 1879, Whistler took his new muse, Maud Franklin to Venice with him, but abandoned her to marry Beatrix Godwin, the wealthy widow of his architect friend E.W. Godwin, in 1888.

BOTH Hassam and Whistler were born in Massachusetts, cradle of the American revolution. Hassam was back in Boston after a few years in Paris, but Whistler never returned to his homeland after arriving in Paris in 1855.

LIKE Monet, Hassam adored the colour and movement of flags. His picture Allies Day, 1917, showing a flag-begirt avenue owes much to Monet's *Rue Montorgueil decked out with flags* (1878).

FREDERICK CHILDE HASSAM

1859 - 1935

FREDERICK CHILDE HASSAM was born in Dorchester, Massachusetts, USA in 1859. After training as a painter, printmaker and wood carver, he travelled to Paris and stayed there from 1886 to 1889. He lived near the Café Guerbois, and mingled with the circle of artists who regularly met there. Profoundly influenced by Impressionism, he returned to the USA intent on using the precepts and techniques he had learnt in Paris to capture the exhilarating city life of New York and Boston. He also painted seascapes of the New England coast.

Hassam was a member of the group of American Impressionists calling themselves The Ten. He died in 1935.

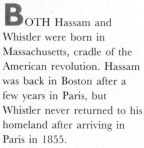

SEPTEMBER
29
30
NOTES

IMPROVISATION (1899)
Childe Hassam

66

There are days here [New York] when the skies and the atmosphere are exactly those of Paris and when the squares and parks are every bit as beautiful in colours and grouping.

HASSAM

99

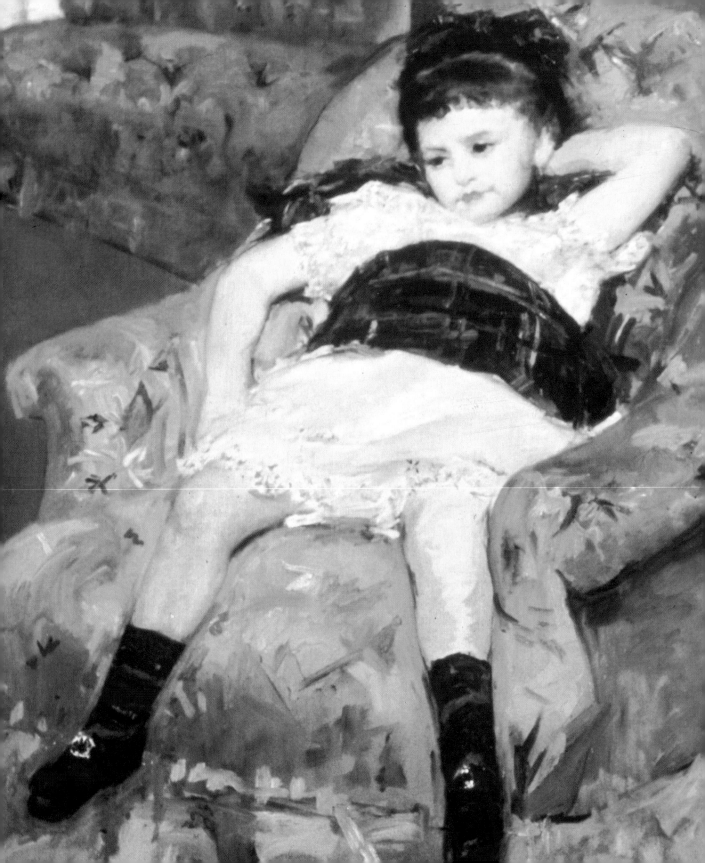

October

MARY STEVENSON CASSATT

1844 - 1926

MARY CASSATT was born in Allegheny City, Philadelphia, USA in 1844. Her father was a banker and mayor of his city and was wealthy enough to take his family for extended European tours. They travelled in France and Germany between 1850 and 1855, spending much of their time in Paris. When she was 16, Cassatt studied at the Pennsylvania Academy of Fine Arts, but became frustrated with this over academic regime and went to Paris to study in 1865. Working with Couture (who had taught Manet) and in the Louvre, Cassatt had moderate success and her work *The Mandolin Player* was accepted in the Salon of 1868. After a period of travelling and studying in Italy, Spain and the Netherlands, she finally settled permanently in Paris in 1875. She knew Monet, Renoir, Morisot, Manet and Sisley, but her guiding light was Degas, whom she met in 1877. He invited her to show her work in the Exhibition of 1879, and she aligned herself with the Impressionists sharing their dislike of the Salon and their enthusiasm for contemporary subjects.

Cassatt worked in oils, pastels and drypoint, a form of printmaking, and held her first one-woman show in November 1893. As had Morisot, she found that her subject matter was circumscribed by convention, but her pictures of woman and children reflect a self-absorbed, enigmatic dignity rather than indulgent sentimentality. A brilliant conversationalist, widely read in French literature, Cassatt also advised her rich American friends about art buying in Europe, and was instrumental in introducing Impressionism to the new world. In 1904, the French government made her a Chevalier of the Légion d'Honneur. After 1908, she never left France again and died in 1926.

RED ALIZAR'

YELLOW OCHRE

VERMILION

COBALT VIOLET

COBALT BLUE

IVORY BLACK

LEAD WHITE

LITTLE GIRL IN A BLUE ARMCHAIR *Mary Stevenson Cassatt*

OCTOBER

1

2

3

NOTES

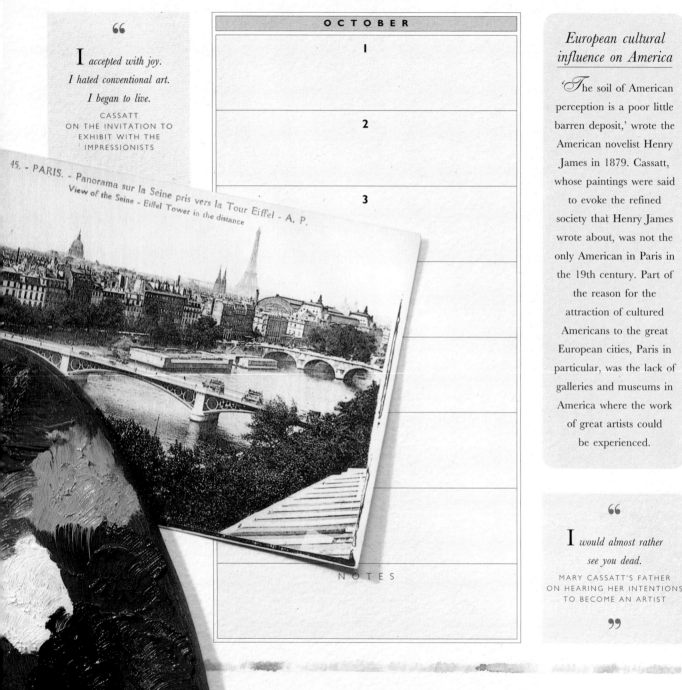

45. - PARIS. - Panorama sur la Seine pris vers la Tour Eiffel - A. P.
View of the Seine - Eiffel Tower in the distance

European cultural influence on America

'*The* soil of American perception is a poor little barren deposit,' wrote the American novelist Henry James in 1879. Cassatt, whose paintings were said to evoke the refined society that Henry James wrote about, was not the only American in Paris in the 19th century. Part of the reason for the attraction of cultured Americans to the great European cities, Paris in particular, was the lack of galleries and museums in America where the work of great artists could be experienced.

OCTOBER
8
9
1 0
1 1
1 2
1 3
1 4
NOTES

N 1890, the exhibition of Japanese art at the École des Beaux Arts electrified Paris. Particularly attractive to the Impressionist in general, and Cassatt in particular, were the Ukiyo-e prints that depicted 'scenes from the floating world,' the fleeting activities of everyday life. The flat, decorative colours and expressive lines were very influential.

OCTOBER
15
16
17
18
19
20
21
NOTES

OCTOBER

22

1906 Cézanne *dies*

23

24

25

26

27

28

NOTES

Degas and Cassatt

'*I* used to go and flatten my nose against that window and absorb all I could of his art. It changed my life. I saw art then as I wanted to see it.' Cassatt met Degas in 1877, and he became a friend and mentor from then on. Both were independent-minded and had their occasional 'spicy estrangements' but they remained close for the rest of their lives.

CASSATT was always interested in the printmaking process. In 1879 she bought her own press and showed prints in the 1880 Impressionists Exhibition. She was particularly keen on a process called drypoint, in which the artist draws directly onto the metal plate with a hard steel point. The raised edge, known as the burr, left by the point carries the ink. This flattens out after many impressions, so editions are limited.

'IT has been one of the chief things in my life to help fine things across the Atlantic.' After persuading her heiress friend Louisine Havemeyer to buy Degas' pastel *The Ballet Rehearsal*, the first Impressionist work ever to go to the USA, Cassatt used her skill and artistic connections to help other Americans assemble impressive collections of European art. The Havemeyer Impressionist collection, formed under Cassatt's expert eye, was bequeathed to the Metropolitan Museum of Modern Art in New York.

CASSATT travelled alone in Spain in 1872–3 visiting Madrid and Seville, and returned there in 1883 with her mother. Like Manet, Cassatt was profoundly influenced by Velásquez, and some of her Spanish paintings were accepted for the Salon.

In 1875, writing home to her sister Louisa, May Alcott described Cassatt as 'a woman of real genius, she will be a first class light as soon as her pictures get a little circulated and known, for they are handled in such a masterly way, with a touch of strength one seldom finds coming from a woman's fingers.'

OCTOBER

29

30

1839 Sisley *born*

31

NOTES

HER female figures are dignified, almost enigmatic, absorbed in their own actions. They appear caught unawares, much as Degas' women do, not self-consciously posed but living their lives.

CASSATT'S best known paintings were made after her parents and sister came to live with her, providing a constant source of models and intimate, blameless domestic rituals – such as five o' clock tea – for her to paint.

November

CAMILLE PISSARRO

1830 - 1903

VIRIDIAN

EMERALD GREEN

CADMIUM YELLOW

VERMILION

CAMILLE PISSARRO was born in 1830 in St Thomas, West Indies, into a well-to-do business family. At the age of 11, Pissarro was sent to Paris to school, where he neglected his studies in favour of drawing. He returned to join his father's business in 1847, where he used the margin in the inventory ledgers to sketch the dockers unloading goods. Five years later, he met Fritz Melbye, a Danish artist commissioned to record the plant and animal life of the Caribbean, who invited him to South America to help him. On his return from Caracas, Pissarro's father agreed to support him while he studied art and in 1855, he arrived in Paris, just in time to see the exhibition at the Paris World Fair. Impressed by Corot's work, he went to see the artist himself, who offered advice and help, as did Anton Melbye, the brother of Fritz. In 1857, Pissarro studied at the Académie Suisse, where he met Monet, whose radiant colours influenced him to change his own palette. He showed in the Salon in 1859, in the Salon des Refusés of 1863 and in all eight Impressionist exhibitions, but for the next 30 years, his life was very hard as he faced crippling poverty and his work was derided.

COBALT BLUE

RED ALIZARIN LAKE

Pissarro's preferred subject was country life, which he painted with a directness that avoided allegory or symbolism; he had a profound and intimate feeling for nature. Most of all he was a painter of light. Staunch, generous, sane and humble, Pissarro was the lynch pin of the Impressionists. Although constant to his own art, he was always open to new ideas and always ready to communicate his own discoveries. Courageous in adversity and enthusiastic to the last, he died in 1903.

ULTRAMARINE

COBALT VIOLET

ZINC WHITE

RED ROOFS, CORNER OF THE VILLAGE IN WINTER *Camille Pissarro*

THE most exotic of the Impressionists, Pissarro was born at Charlotte-Amalie, the capital of St Thomas in the Danish Antilles. His father, a French jew from Bordeaux, and his mother, of Spanish Creole origin, ran a highly successful import-export business and store.

DURING the Franco-Prussian war, when his home at Louveciennes was overrun by soldiers and much of his work destroyed, Pissarro sent his wife and child to the safety of the south of France and went to England to stay with his mother in Upper Norwood just outside London. He did not think much of it: 'What a difference I find here. One meets only disdain, indifference, even rudeness...' However, he went back again in 1890 to paint *The Serpentine, Hyde Park, Effects of Fog* and *The Bridge at Charing Cross* and in 1892 to paint a series on Kew Gardens.

After 1890, Pissarro's eye was infected and he had to go indoors to paint. He did this by standing at the window of Nadar, the Parisian photographer, who often let his studio be used for exhibitions.

NOVEMBER

1

2

3

4

5

6

7

NOTES

Public

'**Y**OU must go to the countryside. The muse is in the woods.' This was Corot's advice to Pissarro and he never forgot it. Until bad health stopped him, he would paint outside, and was a familiar sight to the farmers of the Vexin loping across the meadows with a stick in one hand and his easel over his shoulder. Even in Paris he was indefatigable, striding about Montmartre from his studio to the Café Guerbois.

NOVEMBER
8
9
10
11
12
13

1903 Pissarro *dies*

1840 Monet *born*

TES

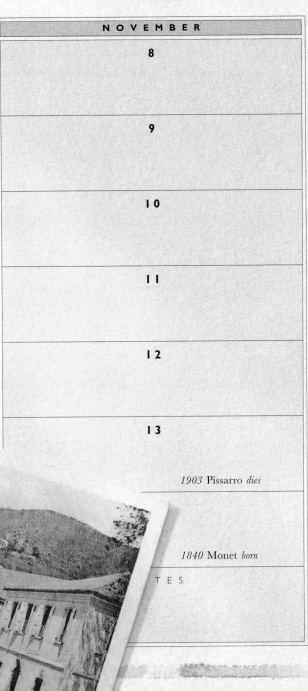

St. Thomas

The Vexin

The Vexin lies between the Normandy coast and the Seine. Many of the Impressionists painted and lived there; Monet lived at Giverny, Renoir at La Roche-Guyon and Morisot bought a country house at Le Mesnil near Juziers, but Pissarro made it his own. The Pissarros lived in Pontoise from 1867-9 then again from 1872-1882. Pissarro persuaded the restless Cézanne to bring his wife and new baby to Pontoise in 1872, and they later moved to nearby Auvers. In 1882, Pissarro found the house at Eragny-sur-Epte which was to be his permanent home. The two artists worked side by side for five years. Cézanne mellowed under Pissarro's paternal approval and they helped each other to refine their work. 'He was influenced by me and I by him,' wrote Pissarro. Critics agree that these years were Pissarro's best creative period.

LES LAVANDIÈRES
Camille Pissarro

> A *beautiful painting by this artist is the act of an honest man. I could not define his talent better than that.*
> ÉMILE ZOLA

NOVEMBER
1 5
1 6
1 7
1 8
1 9
2 0
2 1
N O T E S

Virgulisme

*I*n 1884, when Pissarro was uncharacteristically depressed about his progress, he met Seurat and Signac. Their elaborate theory of pointillism, or divisionism, rekindled his enthusiasm, and for some years he followed their precepts, painting with small, comma-like strokes in a style known as virgulisme. However, it proved too cerebral and restrictive for his broad talent and he returned to his picturesque style in 1890.

> *Everything is beautiful, the important thing is to know how to interpret it.*
>
> PISSARRO

PISSARRO was as prolific with his engravings as he was with his paintings. He made etchings, engravings, aquatints and drypoints and like Degas, developed a personal style. He worked on etchings throughout his career, but only began printing his own in 1890.

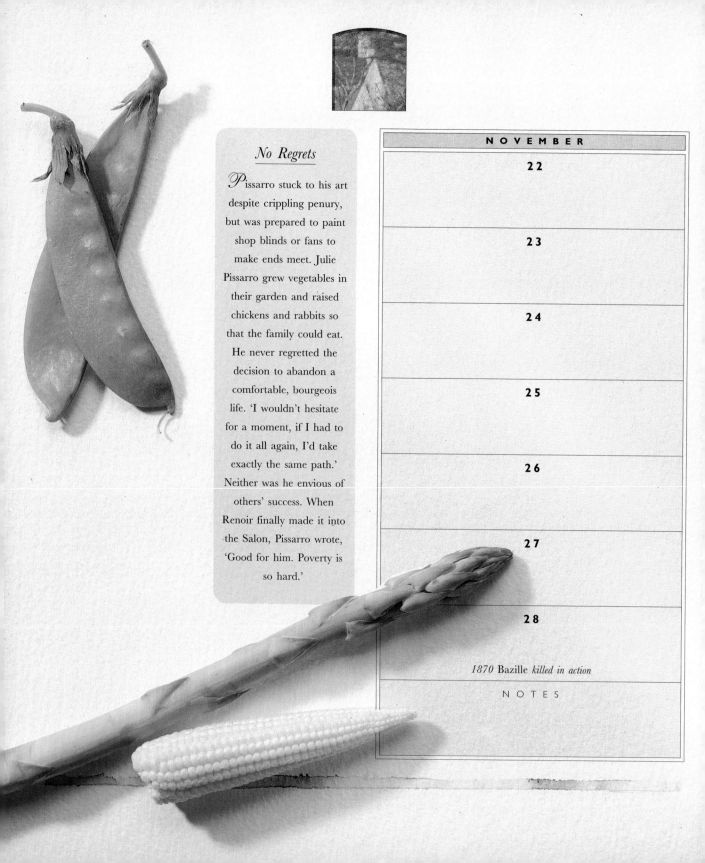

No Regrets

℘issarro stuck to his art despite crippling penury, but was prepared to paint shop blinds or fans to make ends meet. Julie Pissarro grew vegetables in their garden and raised chickens and rabbits so that the family could eat. He never regretted the decision to abandon a comfortable, bourgeois life. 'I wouldn't hesitate for a moment, if I had to do it all again, I'd take exactly the same path.' Neither was he envious of others' success. When Renoir finally made it into the Salon, Pissarro wrote, 'Good for him. Poverty is so hard.'

NOVEMBER

22

23

24

25

26

27

28

1870 Bazille *killed in action*

NOTES

NOVEMBER
29
30
31
NOTES

Death of a Dear One

*I*n 1874, Pissarro's
only daughter
Jeanne, known as
Minette, died
at the age of 9. Pissarro
rarely painted portraits
but he did paint
one of his little
girl which may have
been some comfort to the
family after their
tragic loss.

"

*S*adness, bitterness, pain I
can forget about, even ignore,
in the joy of work. Suffering
only grabs hold of the lazy . .
PISSARRO

"

December

EDGAR GERMAIN HILAIRE DEGAS

1834 - 1917

DEGAS was born in 1834 in Paris, the son of a wealthy banker Pierre-Auguste de Gas. There was no opposition to his artistic vocation and he studied at the École des Beaux Arts under Lamothe and in Italy. In 1862, he joined the throng of artists copying in the Louvre, where he met Manet who introduced him to the circle of young artists and thinkers who met in the Café Guerbois.

The Impressionist preoccupation with the immediate and contemporary struck a chord with Degas, attracting him to modern subjects – race courses, the theatre, people at work, the heroics of the everyday. However, he had no truck with the *plein air* school of thought: all his work was done in the studio from sketches and notes. Degas was a consummate draughtsman in love with movement. His obsession was to record the human body in motion, the transition between one action and the next, the way human muscles worked together to perform physical tasks. His restless, eclectic mind was open to any influence, from the newly discovered Japanese prints of Hokusai to photography.

Grumpy, quarrelsome, irascible, coruscating with caustic wit, Degas made a formidable and respected guest at the weekly salons of fellow artists and intellectuals. His curmudgeonly persona may have been constructed to keep people away from his dust-encrusted Montmartre studio, so he could be alone with his first passion, his work. For the last 20 years of his life he was almost blind (he took up wax modelling as he could not see well enough to paint), reclusive and solitary. He died in 1917.

VERMILION

IVORY BLACK

ZINC WHITE

PRUSSIAN BLUE

VIRIDIAN

NAPLES YELLOW

RED EARTH

YELLOW OCHRE

RAW UMBER

THE DANCING CLASS *Edgar Degas*

DEGAS' paintings of ballet dancers and the theatre are possibly his most famous work. However, it was not for love of the dance that he chose them, but because they were moving targets. 'They call me painter of dancers; they don't realize that for me the dancer is a pretext for painting pretty materials and rendering movements.'

MANET took Degas to the races at Longchamp, and he never looked back. Attracted by the colour and movement, the spectacle of human and animal in motion, Degas made many race course paintings, the most extraordinary of which is *At the Races* (1869–72).

66

H*e is a terrible man, but frank and loyal.*
PISSARRO

99

DECEMBER

1	
2	
3	*1903* Renoir *dies*
4	
5	*1926* Monet *dies* *1841* Bazille *born*
6	
7	

NOTES

DECEMBER

8

9

10

11

12

14

NOTES

Opera Buff

*F*amily wealth meant that the young Degas led a life of cultured aristocratic ease. He regularly attended the opera and dined with its stars and celebrities. Concerts were held at the Degas home every Monday. After 1875, the wealth was lost and the society gentlemen had to transform himself into the working artist, which he did with great success.

PARIS. — L'Opéra.

DEGAS often used a technique called *peinture à l'essence*, in which oil is removed from the pigment which is then thinned with turpentine to make it dry more quickly. When oil painting, he would often smear the paint on with his hands and fingers, then finish the work with a brush.

DECEMBER

15

16

17

18

19

20

21

NOTES

EVER the experimenter, Degas devised the monotype, a mixture of painting, pastel and engraving techniques. Applying ink directly to an unblemished etching plate, he made prints of the result, and then used these as a basis for pastel or oil compositions.

'Pastel very lightly applied to a somewhat glossy paper is very vibrant. It is a beautiful medium.' Degas made endless experiments with pastels, mixing them with water, gouache, or thinned oils to create different effects.

DECEMBER
2 2
2 3
2 4
2 5
2 6
2 7
1873 Société Anonyme Cooperative des Artistes, Peintres, Sculpteurs, Graveurs etc *formed*
2 8
N O T E S

WHEN his friend and pupil Mary Cassatt took Degas to the milliners with her, he was fascinated by the gestures women make when concentrating on their work. A series of paintings showing scenes at milliner shops rank alongside Degas' series of laundresses.

IN 1880, Kodak introduced the first portable camera, and Degas seized upon this new invention with enthusiasm. He photographed all his friends and relations and supervised the printing of his negatives. The composition of many of his paintings already showed photographic features such as the abrupt cropping of the image, the manipulation of artificial light sources, close-ups and unlikely points of view.

AROUND 1856,
The engraver Félix
Braquemond discovered the
series of Japanese Hokusai
prints that were to take Paris
by storm. Degas was greatly
influenced by the subject
matter and the way gestures
and movement were
conveyed.

DEGAS' mother,
Marie-Céléstine Musson, was
a Creole, born in New
Orleans. To recuperate after
his shattering experiences in
the Franco-Prussian war,
Degas visited his relations in
his mother's native city and
painted 15 paintings,
including *The Cotton
Exchange in New Orleans* (1873)
which shows his brothers
Achille and René and his
uncle Michel Musson,
among others.

66

DEGAS SPEAKING

99

*Do you know what I think of painters
who work in country lanes?
If I were the government I would have a special police squad
to keep an eye on people who do landscapes from life.*

———— o ————

*There is love and there is work,
and we have but one heart.*

———— o ————

*I should like to be famous
and unknown.*

———— o ————

*A picture is an original combination
of lines and tones that set each other off.*

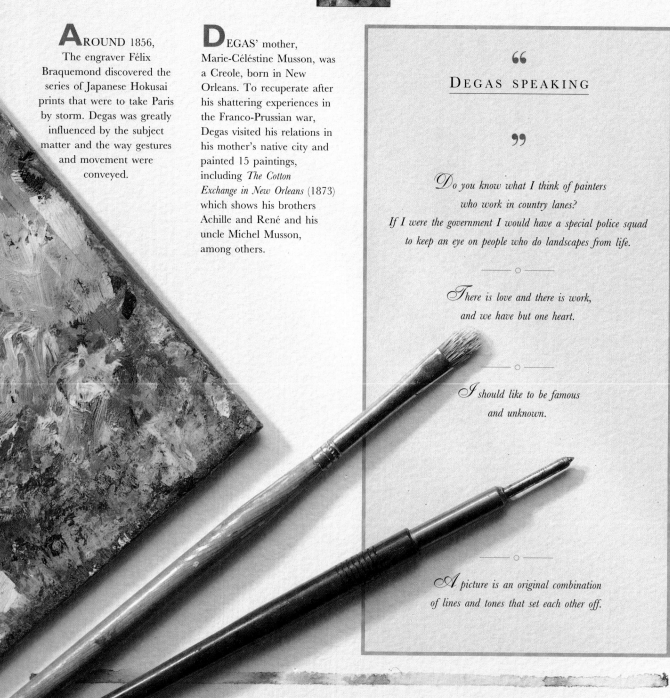

DURING the French revolution, Degas' grandfather had fled to Italy and married into a Neapolitan family. Between 1854 and 1860, young Degas regularly visited his relations in Naples, Rome and Florence, where he was able to study the work of the Old Masters at first hand. His *Portrait of the Bellelli Family* (1860-62) is an austere study of his aunt, Baroness Bellelli, and her daughters.

DEGAS was a bachelor, but sometimes speculated wistfully about finding 'a nice little wife, simple and quiet' and some children. He never did, but had many women friends including Mary Cassatt and later Suzanne Valadon, who modelled for Renoir and Toulouse-Lautrec, and became a successful artist herself.

WHEN his sight became too feeble to paint, Degas turned to modelling in wax, making models of dancers and horses. These were later cast in bronze (some after his death). *The Little Dancer* (1880-81) with her real tutu is the best known.

DECEMBER

29

30

31

NOTES

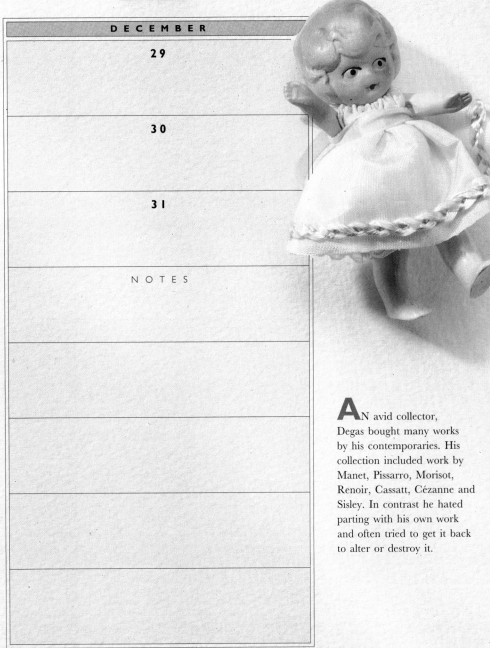

AN avid collector, Degas bought many works by his contemporaries. His collection included work by Manet, Pissarro, Morisot, Renoir, Cassatt, Cézanne and Sisley. In contrast he hated parting with his own work and often tried to get it back to alter or destroy it.

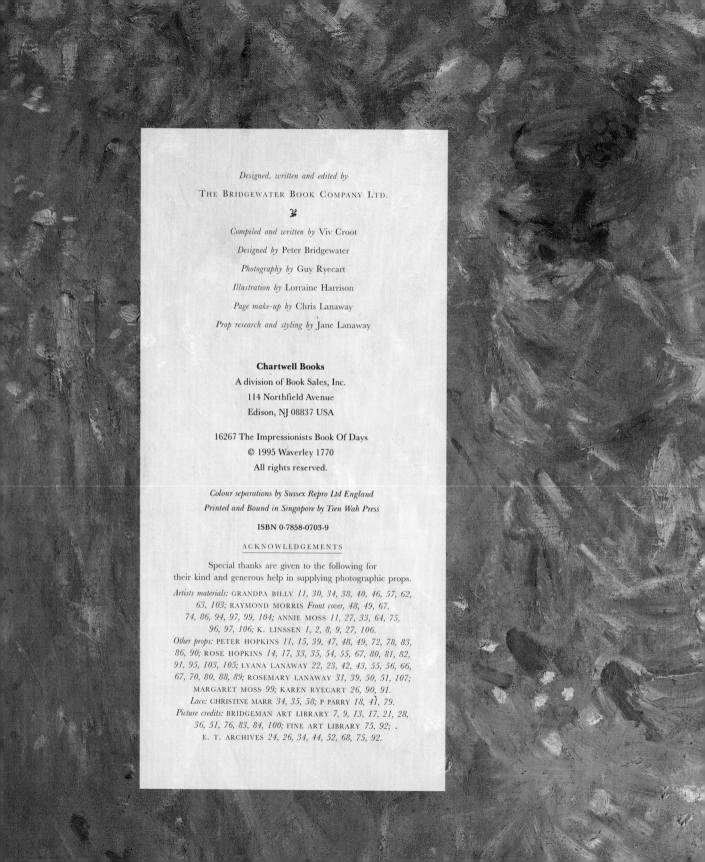

Designed, written and edited by

THE BRIDGEWATER BOOK COMPANY LTD.

❧

Compiled and written by Viv Croot

Designed by Peter Bridgewater

Photography by Guy Ryecart

Illustration by Lorraine Harrison

Page make-up by Chris Lanaway

Prop research and styling by Jane Lanaway

Chartwell Books

A division of Book Sales, Inc.

114 Northfield Avenue

Edison, NJ 08837 USA

16267 The Impressionists Book Of Days

© 1995 Waverley 1770

Colour separations by Sussex Repro Ltd England

Printed and Bound in Singapore by Tien Wah Press

ISBN 0-7858-0703-9

ACKNOWLEDGEMENTS

Special thanks are given to the following for
their kind and generous help in supplying photographic props.

Artists materials: GRANDPA BILLY *11, 30, 34, 38, 40, 46, 57, 62,
63, 103;* RAYMOND MORRIS *Front cover, 48, 49, 67,
74, 86, 94, 97, 99, 104;* ANNIE MOSS *11, 27, 33, 64, 75,
96, 97, 106;* K. LINSSEN *1, 2, 8, 9, 27, 106.*

Other props: PETER HOPKINS *11, 15, 39, 47, 48, 49, 72, 78, 83,
86, 90;* ROSE HOPKINS *14, 17, 33, 35, 54, 55, 67, 80, 81, 82,
91, 95, 103, 105;* LYANA LANAWAY *22, 23, 42, 43, 55, 56, 66,
67, 70, 80, 88, 89;* ROSEMARY LANAWAY *31, 39, 50, 51, 107;*
MARGARET MOSS *99;* KAREN RYECART *26, 90, 91.*

Lace: CHRISTINE MARR *34, 35, 58;* P PARRY *18, 41, 79.*

Picture credits: BRIDGEMAN ART LIBRARY *7, 9, 13, 17, 21, 28,
36, 51, 76, 83, 84, 100;* FINE ART LIBRARY *75, 92;* .
E. T. ARCHIVES *24, 26, 34, 44, 52, 68, 75, 92.*

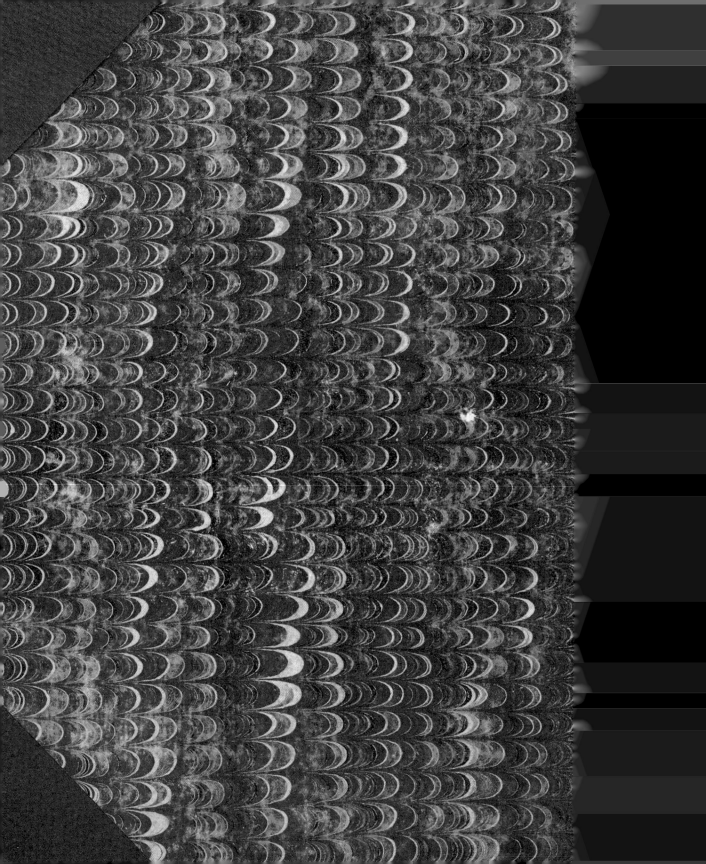